Generis
PUBLISHING

Articulating the Shan migrant community in Thai society through community radio

A case study of the Map Radio FM 99 in the city of Chiang Mai, Thailand

Hyeonsoo Jeon

Title: Articulating the Shan migrant community in Thai society through community radio

A case study of the Map Radio FM 99 in the city of Chiang Mai, Thailand

ISBN: 979-8-88676-656-1

Author: Hyeonsoo Jeon

Cover image: www.pixabay.com

Publisher: Generis Publishing
Online orders: www.generis-publishing.com
Contact email: info@generis-publishing.com

Abstract

Community media as an alternative public sphere for minorities has emerged apart from mainstream media and formal public spheres. Its ethos of understanding community participation as a key component of operating a station highlights its potential to empower community members as active social agents. This study examines the social consequences of an ethnic migrant community radio station, Map Radio FM 99, to explore its role for the Shan migrant community in Chiang Mai, Thailand. Employing a qualitative approach, this study found that participation in community radio helps participants to be socially active in Thai society by maximising their participation in the social sphere through media. This study concludes that participation in Map Radio enables the Shan migrant community to better adapt to Thai society by providing and obtaining information necessary for their lives in Thailand and by contributing to the formation of a collective identity as ethnic migrant workers, thereby creating community cohesion. Nonetheless, lack of political efficacy due to the challenging political environment in Thailand might partly prevent Map Radio from completely functioning as an alternative public sphere. Lastly, it is essential to understand that the current trend of community broadcasting services are moving forward to keep up with changing environments due to digital transformation such as an innovative delivery of online broadcasting services. In consideration of this change in mind, MAP Radio has been pioneering the community media landscape in Thailand as the first and the most recognized channel for the Shan migrant community in Chiang Mai.

__Keywords__: community radio, alternative public sphere, behavioral economics, sustainability, digital governance, ethnic migrant, social participation, Thailand, community cohesion.

Table of Contents

1. Introduction

Media in the public sphere plays an important role in ensuring citizens' participation in modern society. The public sphere indicates a communicative space where citizens raise their opinions, interests and discourses with freedom of expression free from external powers (Habermas, Lennox, & Lennox, 1974). In particular, the importance of the public sphere arises from its contributing role of achieving social integration through facilitation of public discussion. However, a general disregard in mainstream media for minorities often limits their opportunities to participate in the public sphere and leads to their exclusion from society (Atton, 2001). In response to this crisis, community media emerge as an alternative public sphere from mainstream and commercial media. Emphasising community participation at the grassroots level, community media highlights its potential to empower community members and promote democratic communication across many spheres of society.

The growth of community media is closely linked with increasing migration patterns worldwide (Georgiou, 2005). Such presence of community media appears in Thailand, a multicultural society where approximately 70 ethnic groups co-exist (Jory, 2000; Hayami, 2006). Geographic proximity and cultural similarities of northern Thailand and Myanmar as well as the recent economic growth in Thailand have attracted Shan migrants for decades (Jirattikorn, 2016; IOM, 2013). However, their disadvantaged legal and economic status leads to their occupation of the most marginalised sections of Thai society and their exclusion from the public sphere (Murakami, 2012). Furthermore, Thai media has often described Burmese migrant workers as illegal or a threat to national security (Sunpuwan & Niyomsilpa, 2012). Nonetheless, their participation in community

7

radio indicates the creation of an alternative public sphere for the migrant community in a new society. This study understands community radio as a social practice as well as an empowering tool for development intervention. Through a case study of Map Radio FM 99 in Chiang Mai, Thailand, I aim to explore community radio functions as an alternative public sphere and facilitates social participation for the Shan migrant community in this book.

2. The emergence of community media

This chapter provides a literature review examining historical and conceptual approaches to community media. I first explore the connection between media and development from a historical and international perspectives, examining how this connection affected the emergence of community media characterised by alternative and participatory natures. Community radio is one form of community media, so it is important to understand community media broadly (Bosch 2014). Second, I introduce the notion of the public sphere in relation to community media and the exclusion of minorities. Third, I discuss the elusiveness of both 'community' and community media run by minorities. Finally, I examine the status of community radio in Thailand and existing literature on the social consequences of community media on a global level.

2.1. Historical connection between media and development

Historically, the connection between media and development traces back to the 1950s, post-World War II. Media was expected to play a role in facilitating development as a method of transforming knowledge and ideas from modernised countries to developing countries (Mefalopulos 2008; McCall 2011). However, this provoked a perception of cultural imperialism in developing countries and perpetuated the top-down use of media as a tool for expressing a country's slogan on a national level. The emergence of a participatory communication paradigm pushed back against one-way communication and gave birth to two- way communication flows (Servaes & Malikhao 2005). Participatory approaches in particular saw community as a necessary element for producing media because the community is well-attuned to daily issues (*ibid.*). Accordingly, in this approach, both community and individual members are seen as actives agents for achieving developmental efforts.

In the meantime, against cultural imperialism, international players in media expressed concerns about achieving democratic communication. Such concerns are expressed in the United Nations Educational, Scientific and Cultural Organization (UNESCO)'s report on the structural reform of global communication infrastructure (MacBride 1980). Even though this reform was confined to national governmental levels, this inspired local and global civil society to contribute to so-called 'globalization from below' with the support of communication rights in the 1990s (Saeed 2009, 469). According to World Association of Christian Communicators (2006),

> Communication rights go beyond mere freedom of opinion and expression, to include areas such as democratic media governance, participation in one's own culture, linguistic rights, rights to enjoy the fruits of human creativity, to education, to privacy, peaceful assembly, and self-determination. These are questions of inclusion and exclusion, of quality and accessibility. In short, they are questions of human dignity. (67)

Such an assertion suggests that civil society understands communication rights as basic human rights. Nevertheless, a growing worldwide recognition of communication rights does not necessarily guarantee that they are upheld within the boundaries of nation-states (O'Siochru 2004). Arguably, communication rights cannot be fully realised without community media created by an 'alternative communication infrastructure' (Saeed 2009, 470).

2.2. Participatory and alternative community media

The participatory approach discussed in the previous section resulted in many community-led development projects, especially in the global South (Mefalopulos 2008). Serving specific communities, community media operates *for, of,* and *by* the community. This highlights the participatory nature of community media. According to Rennie (2006, 22), community media is broadly defined as 'media that allows for access and participation'. Jankowski (1994, 3) argues that the main differences in community media are attributable to 'the higher level of participation of different social groups and communities'.

It is also possible to understand community media as alternative to mainstream media. Arguably, the growth of community media can be attributed to the inability of mainstream media, public services, and commercial broadcasting to meet the needs of disadvantaged social groups (Lewis 2008). Shukla (2014) claims that mainstream media do not represent the voices of the marginalized. From this perspective, community media are located apart from the state and market and thereby their existence weakens the power of mainstream media (Chiumbu 2014; Conrad 2014). Howley (2005, 2) defines community media as 'grassroots or locally oriented media access initiatives predicated on a profound sense of dissatisfaction with mainstream media form and content, dedicated to the principles of free expression and participatory democracy'. Therefore, community media as an alternative provides marginalized communities with the means to raise their excluded voices (Atton 2001).

Radical media studies, however, argues that alternative media should be replaced with 'citizens' media to prevent the binary notion of community media as alternative which renders ordinary people powerless while providing the elites in

11

mainstream media with absolute power (Rodríguez 2008). Rather, Atton (2001, 21) focuses on the function of community media as complex 'agents of developmental power' which create social participation by producing and disseminating media, more so than in mainstream media, while recognizing their alternative natures simultaneously. Furthermore, he claims that the interest of alternative media is more than simply having an oppositional position to the mainstream media, rather it is 'the processes and relations that form around alternative media' (*ibid.*, 3). This reflects the participatory nature of alternative media, similar to participatory community media.

2.3. Media, the public sphere, and the exclusion of minorities

Media is an essential space for creating public discussion despite divergent opinions among scholars (Butsch 2007; Bosch 2014). In understanding this, the notion of the *public sphere* has been particularly influential. According to Habermas et al. (1974, 49), the public sphere refers to a space where 'citizens behave as a public body when they confer in an unrestricted fashion with the guarantee of freedom of assembly and association and the freedom to express and publish their opinions about matters of general interest'. In principle, this sphere is distinct from the state and the official-economy, thereby enabling citizens to participate independently and equally (*ibid.*). By doing so, the public sphere creates social integration by achieving a single, unitary public sphere from public consensus. This is conducive to a functioning democracy (*ibid.*).

Nevertheless, the concept of the public sphere has been revised and expanded in light of its shortcomings (Fraser 1990; Butsch 2007). Typically, as Fraser (1990) points out, the public sphere proposed by Habermas contributes to the social exclusion of minorities, including women, ethnic groups, and the lower classes.

In other words, in his bourgeois concept of the public sphere, Habermas ignores the existence of minorities who are inherently precluded from the formal public sphere (*ibid.*). In contrast to the public of Habermas' formal public sphere, so-called 'subaltern counterpublics' create alternative public spheres to 'create counter- discourses to formulate oppositional interpretations of their identities, interests, and needs' (*ibid.*, 67).

Community media associated with these subaltern counter-publics are considered important in shaping their identities, needs, and interests, and challenging the dominant order of the formal public sphere. This is well reflected in the statement that

> community media provides a platform for those who are often voiceless in society. Radio, moving image and internet are all powerful campaigning tools to bring attention to inequality and injustice in communities [...] to present their perspectives and challenge negative images of themselves. (Paul Zealey Associates 2007, 5).

2.4. *'Community' media by minorities*

Nevertheless, little research has been completed concerning the use and production of community media by minorities. Moreover, reflecting the diversity of minorities, community media which serves such groups takes on different names, including indigenous, ethnic, migrant, minority, and multicultural media, among others. (Bailey et al 2008; Lin & Song 2006; Mahlanga 2015; Matsaganis et al. 2010; Meadows 2015; Fleras 2009).

Such breadth in naming is partially attributable to the inherent elusiveness of the concept of *community*. Community has been traditionally recognized in terms of

13

geography and ethnicity, examining collective identity and group relations (Carpentier et al. 2003). However, the concept has developed into a fluid notion which encompasses a group of people sharing interests and virtual spaces influenced by the development of information communication technologies (ICTs) (*ibid.*). On the other hand, Cohen (1985, 70) emphasizes the subjective meaning of community, arguing that 'a shift away from the structure of community towards a symbolic construction of community and in order to do so, takes culture, rather than structure as point of departure'. Bosch (2014) asserts that, in the context of community radio, the notion of community should be defined by the changes of the radio station based on their network sociality.

2.5. *Community radio landscape in Thailand*

The presence of community media in Thailand has increased because of continuous political instability, mainly caused by military intervention and the following reaction from civil society called the 'Campaign for Popular Media Reform' (CPMR) in the late 1990s (Klangnarong 2009; Siriyuvasak 2009). According to Booten & Klangnarong (2009), not only the CPMR, but also ethnic minorities, and labour organizations worked together to defend their communication rights and freedom of expression (*ibid.*). Along with increased funding from international donors directed towards Thailand at the time, this social movement resulted in a nationwide surge of community radio. In Thailand, radio is the second most popular medium and almost half of the urban populations listen to the radio (*ibid.*). Lewis (2006) argues that radio was the only medium available for civil society reformers because it is not capital-intensive. Additionally, the 1997 Constitution, which changed the status of frequencies from government resources to national assets, is considered a critical turning point in the spread of community radio in the country (Magpanthong & McDaniel 2015).

14

Before this point, media outlets were mostly controlled by the state and focused largely on the capital city, Bangkok.

Community radio is relatively new in parts of Southeast Asia compared to other developing countries such as those in Africa or Latin America (Helbardt 2015). Though Thailand has the largest number of Community Radio Stations (CRSs) in the region, and there have been several developmental projects concerning community radio (Green 2013; Buckley 2011), community radio has largely been exploited as a tool for political propaganda and profit (Magpanthong & McDaniel 2011; Brooten & Klangnarong 2009). For this reason, the principles of community radio, such as serving the community and non-profits, have been neither strictly nor strongly upheld in the country. Today, no strong legal identity or licensing framework exists for community broadcasting. Moreover, military coups in 2006 and 2014 endangered the status of CRSs and restricted freedom of expression (AMARC 2014). Some scholars doubt whether CRSs exist which aim to empower minorities in Thailand (Supadhiloke 2011). In this regard, research on a national level concerning the interrelation of minorities, community radio, and its social consequences is sparse.

2.6. The social consequences of community media by minorities

Globally, some studies on community media used by minorities demonstrate that these communities can bring about a range of social changes. In order to deliver community benefit ultimately for positive social change and also as a public good, community radio broadcasting should be considered as a tool of development (UNESCO 2023; McDonald & Chignell 2023). For instance, in the case of immigrant media, Matsaganis et al.'s (2010, 60-63) study shows that community media provide new immigrants with information such as immigration and citizenship policies which are not offered by mainstream media.

Moreover, Meadows (2015) in his study on indigenous radio in Australia, equates this radio with an indigenous public sphere which has the potential to connect indigenous people with a mainstream public sphere. While these studies express the potential of community media in connecting minority communities with the mainstream society, some studies reveal that community media play a facilitating role in forging community bonds. In a study on British Muslims and their involvement in community media, Bailey et al. (2008) suggests that community media helps the minority group to articulate their identities, simultaneously confirming their differences in the country's multicultural setting. Further, indigenous community radios in Mexico contributed to making socio-cultural cohesion among ethnic groups by subtly changing the dominant cultural order which weighed on indigenous cultures (Rodríguez 2005).

In Thailand, despite its scarcity, some research shows that ethnic minorities have utilised community radio. For instance, Helbardt's research (2015) on Malay Muslim in southern Thailand shows that community radio has contributed to creating a local public sphere for the community by allowing community

16

members to speak their language in the context of a Muslim insurgency. However, the study also revealed that there have been dominant commercial interests, as well as threats from the Thai military (*ibid.*), which fail to preserve the ethos of community media. Acknowledging these political and commercial disturbances in community radio in Thailand, Supadhiloke's (2011) research nonetheless shows that using the participatory features of community radio creates the potential to empower rural people, particularly hill-tribes, as well-informed citizens.

In summary, despite scholarly interest and contributions to understandings of community media and their use by minorities, the concept and social functions of community media are highly elusive (Howley 2010; Carpentier et al. 2003; Atton 2001). The inherent heterogeneity of the concept *community* makes such an understanding even less attainable. Additionally, this elusiveness is also attributable to the fact that community media is already embedded in the social, political, cultural, and economic context of a given society (Atton 2015; Jallow 2012). In this sense, social consequences revealed by researchers cannot be directed applied in different contexts.

Furthermore, in Thailand, though there is a general consensus that political and business interests are prevalent in community radio, evidence concerning community radio as a tool for empowering ethnic minorities in the country, as well global evidence concerning gaps bridged by minorities with mainstream society and the strengthening of cultural identities through participation in community radio, contribute to the positive relevance to this study. Additionally, the exclusion of minorities in the public sphere leads to the creation of an alternative public sphere *of*, *for*, and *by* minorities.

17

3. Theorising community radio as an alternative public sphere

3.1. Understanding community radio as an alternative public sphere

Community radio is often considered the most effective and democratic method of community communication (Vatikiotis, 2005). Compared to mainstream media, community radio has several advantages, including its "more widespread geographic coverage, access to rural and illiterate populations and its ability to broadcast in minority languages" as well as its low operation cost (Bosch, 2014, p. 430). Above all, easy accessibility leads to a favourable environment for minorities to create an alternative public sphere.

The alternative public spheres indicates a communicative space where minorities create their own discourses (Fraser, 1990; Bosch, 2014; Meadows, 2015). In particular, Fraser's recognition of an alternative public sphere is valuable in understanding community radio. She indicates that alternative public spheres are created as a result of social inequality and the exclusion of minorities from the main public sphere (Fraser, 1990). Fraser (2007) pinpoints the importance of "efficacy" in forming an alternative public sphere. Rooted in political theory, the notion suggests the public sphere should be equipped with both "normative legitimacy" and "political efficacy" to have critical mass (Fraser, 2007). While normative legitimacy concerns the inclusiveness of the public in a sphere, political efficacy concerns delivering the will of the public as a form of civil society, which can be further realised in a certain society (Fraser, 2007, p. 8). In this regard, Fraser claims that the (alternative) public sphere can have an influence on social change when it involves the formation of public opinion and decision-making (1990, pp. 89-92). Furthermore, the recognition of an alternative public sphere implies the

18

presence of multiple public spheres in society. According to Fraser, multiple public spheres are preferred and better ensure participatory parity for all, especially in a multicultural society (1990, pp. 65-70). Although this claim is based on the assumption that "multiple public spheres are situated in a single 'structured setting' that advantages some and disadvantages other" (Fraser 1990, p. 68), it is clear that a single unitary public sphere cannot guarantee participation for all.

On the other hand, in considering the presence of multiple public spheres, Keane (1995) expresses a different perspective, arguing that multiple public spheres are created based on 'difference' within public spheres. Keane distinguishes public spheres on a spatial basis: macro public spheres (global and regional levels), meso-public spheres (at the level of the territorial nation-state), and micro-public spheres (sub-state level). Regarding this approach, Vatikiotis (2010, 39) notes that 'this significantly sets a dynamic understanding of the public sphere on the grounds of practices realized in the arena of civil society'.

According to Keane (1995), a micro public sphere is a local space where the public can easily come for discussions as well as the origin of all social movements. While a meso-public sphere encompasses millions of people as an audience within a national boundary, a macro-public spheres encompasses more than hundreds of millions of people as a consequence of the international concentration of mass media beyond a national level (ibid.). Therefore, community radio is considered part of a micro public sphere as a result of its locality and limited focus. Nevertheless, Keane claims that multiple public spheres are 'complex mosaic of differently sized, overlapping and interconnected public spheres' (ibid., 1). In the current study, I understand community radio as an alternative public sphere which is one of multiple public spheres, drawing on Fraser (1990) and Keane (1995). In this regard, its potential growth and interconnectedness with other public spheres are discussed.

3.2. Participation with different action rationales

In community radio, different forms of participation are made through the different action rationales of participants. For Leal (2009), different action rationales refer to "the differing orientations that motivate the actions of the actors who perform in the space of the radio station, namely the host/presenters and directors who are connected to the station by means of voluntary and contractual regimes" (p.159).

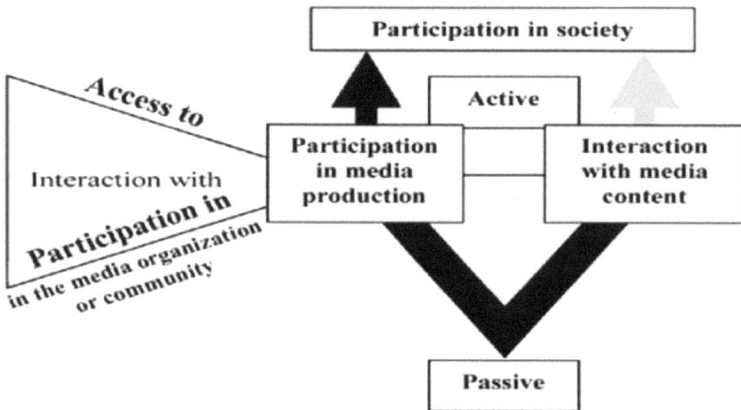

Figure 1. Participation dimensions in the media sphere (Carpentier 2011, p. 70)

As shown in Figure 1 above, Carpentier (2011, p. 67) argues that audience participation in media can take two forms: participation *through* media and participation *in* media. According to Carpentier (2011), participation through

20

media takes the form of expressing individual voices and experiences to interact with other people. In addition, participation in media production consists of content-related participation and structural participation (Carpentier, 2011). While the former refers to direct engagement in the production of media content, the latter refers to involvement in decision-making processes. Both forms of participation encourage participants to be active in the public spheres related to their daily lives (Carpentier, 2011). Arguably, both participation in media production and interaction with media content ultimately lead to participation in society (Figure 1).

3.3. Strategic alliances and partnerships

Partnership and strategic alliances between community media and other organizations are considered important as they help produce social gain (Lewis 2008; Holwey 2010). Theoretically, such social gain can be understood through a consideration of the rhizome as postulated by Deleuze and Guattari. According to Deleuze and Guattari (1987), the rhizome encompasses a philosophy of the state of being non-linear, anarchic, and nomadic. They argue that the rhizome 'ceaselessly established connections between semiotic chains, organizations of power and circumstances' (Carpentier et al. 2003, 61). With this metaphor, it can be seen that community media can make a fluid connection with the state and the market but can also act as a part of civil society (*ibid.*). Additionally, Bosch (2014, 428) notes that the rhizome helps community radio to 'create linkages within and between communities and leads to horizontal growth through its grassroots engagement with community organizations and community members'.

Carpentier et al. (2003, 51) asserts that "the antagonism towards state and market and the resistance against a multitude of hegemonic discourses has left the community movement in a position of discursive isolation." From this point of view, different types of partnerships or strategic alliances are recommended. According to Carpentier et al. (2003), strategic alliances reduce the long-standing antagonism of community media towards mainstream media. Furthermore, partnerships with civic groups can facilitate social movements through common goals (*ibid.*).

According to Girard (2007, 16), partnerships in community radio are 'a result of an association with a Non-Governmental Organization (NGO), profession, business or government agency outside of the station'. Through partnership, community radio can have partnership volunteers and partner organizations. Partner organizations often decide to partner with radio stations for the purpose of airtime and establishing reciprocal relationships (*ibid.*). Community radio is characterized by a high level of volunteer participation because of its non-profit ethos (Bonin & Opoku-Mensah 1998; Girard 2007; Bosch 2014). Volunteers can be considered as individual volunteers or partnership volunteers (Girard 2007). While individual volunteers participate in community radio within the community, partnership volunteers come to the station through external organizations which are partners of a radio station. There is a general perception that partnership volunteers have a higher level of expertise than individual volunteers who are more enthusiastic to participate (*ibid.*).

Work by Bailey et al. (2008, 156) notes that collaboration with public and mainstream media can be beneficial if this collaboration is based on respect for the individual actors involved. Additionally, such collaboration may strengthen the relatively weak position of community media, broadening 'public sphericules' (ibid.). However, 'public sphericules' should be differentiated from counter-publics in the alternative public sphere. Pulblic sphericules are 'social fragments that do not have critical mass' (Cunningham 2010, 134), which has 'limited chances to get proper attention and have a minimal effect on national politics' (Lee 2013, 2612). Members of spericules do not have much interest in participating in other public spheres (Lee 2013). Cunningmham (2010) explains that the development of ICTs along with globalisation enables communities to find their community members beyond the nation and stay closer with them within this community. For this reason, while counter-publics attempt to make connections with other public spheres, public sphericules rarely interact with other spheres, persisting in their own differences (Lee 2013). With a similar perspective, Schiller (2007) claims that the presence of multiple alternative public spheres (made by partnerships or strategic alliances) does not necessarily result in favourable conditions for social inclusion. The question here is whether strategic alliances or partnerships facilitate the character of public sphericules or counter-publics in community radio.

3.4. The socio-cultural functions of community radio

Community radio, participation, and empowerment

Entering public discourses through participation in community radio promotes a greater level of individual and collective agency (Berrigan 1981). Agency is a central concept to understand empowerment, describing the process of change, whereas an agent is someone 'who acts and brings about social change' (Sen 2001; Kabeer 2012).

Describing community radio as empowerment radio, Jallov (2012) explains that empowerment grows when people realize their knowledge and through the power obtained by sharing this knowledge with others. Similarly, Khawaja (2005) argues that empowerment consists of information and influence. The first component of empowerment, *information*, can be divided into two aspects, provision of information and access to information. While the provision of information intends to benefit listeners by matching their needs, access to information does so by allowing them to make informed decisions (*ibid.*). In this sense, participation in community radio can be understood as a means of providing and gaining information (Bosch 2014). Indicating the role of community radio as democratising information, Shukla (2014) claims that information further reduces disparities in resources and opportunities by facilitating their equitable allocation in society at large. The recent COVID-19 pandemic particularly highlighted the importance of information sharing and also media and information literacy for the public to prevent misleading the vulnerable population among the community (UNDP 2021; UNESCO 2020).

Moreover, as discussed by Khwaja (2005), information is often accompanied by influence. *Influence* refers to agents' relative ownership in decision-making

24

processes, largely linked to bargaining power (*ibid.*, 274). The bargaining power might suggest power relationship with others, however, for Page and Czuba (1999), power can also be understood as mutual sharing and collaboration.

In discussing radical democracy, Rodríguez (2008, 21) claims that community radio is a space where 'quotidian politics' can take place in everyday life. Participants in community radio experience a unique setting with 'a more fluid notion of citizenship' (*ibid.*, 160). Similarly, Rennie (2006) suggests that community media provides community members with civic competency outside of formal political structures. The concept of citizenship presented here is not confined to legal statuses or arrangements. According to Kabeer (2012), citizenship can be understood in terms of citizenship as status and citizenship as practice. While the former refers to the legal arrangement of defining citizens' rights and responsibilities, the latter details the ways in which community members seek to act on or challenge formal definitions of citizenship (*ibid.*). Furthermore, Kabeer argues that citizenship as a practice is connected to human agency in terms of interpreting understandings of citizenship (*ibid.*). Therefore, it is likely that the practices of community radio are invested in the process of experiencing citizenship as practice.

Community radio, participation, and collective identity

Community radio enables community members to share a language that reflects their common social and ethnic formation. For Howley (2010), this facilitates the creation of a sense of shared identity and collective solidarity. Especially for minority groups, this can be an act of demonstrating indigenous forms of expression and defending cultural identities (Rodríguez 2008). Nonetheless, the notion of collective identity can present dualistic elements. Identity appears from

25

a dynamic system of relationships and refers not only to inclusion but also to exclusion in defining social boundaries (Lewis 2008). Furthermore, this collective identity differentiates one community from another (Howley 2010). However, in discussing community as 'unity in difference' (Cohen 1985), Howley (2010) explains that while community implies similarities between/within community members through symbolic practices such as language and discursive practices, diverse and heterogeneous lives and experiences exist within community.

3.5. The social consequences of community radio

The practices of community radio result in social consequences for a given society as well as the community. By recognising community media as a form of social capital, Fleras (2009, 2015) argues that community media creates bonding (within a community) and bridges roles (between communities) for migrant communities in a new society. According to Fleras (2009, pp. 726–727), community media can operate inwardly by announcing relevant information about a homeland and outwardly by reporting information of "relevance and immediacy" necessary for life in a new society.

	Reactive	Proactive
Inward focus (bonding/insular)	**Constructing buffers** Reaction to invisibility in mainstream media by offering the perspectives of minorities	**Creating bonds** Foster community pride/cohesion by celebrating community achievements and provide news from homeland
Outward focus (bridging/integrative)	**Removing barriers** Address injustice by advocating for positive change and levelling uneven discourse	**Building bridges** Civic participation while fostering intercultural dialogue for social integration

Table 1. Multidimensionality of community media as social capital
(Source: Fleras 2009, 2015).

Community media can operate reactively and proactively (Fleras, 2009). As alternative media, community media responds to the needs, identities and furthermore, the realities of communities which are not discussed in mainstream media by offering a community's perspectives. Moreover, community media can

27

proactively celebrate community culture and identities to create social cohesion within the community. However, thinking from an outward perspective, such strengthened cohesion may insulate a community from a new society (Fleras, 2009). Nonetheless, Fleras (Fleras, 2009, p. 726) emphasises that the outward role of community media should not be underestimated because it allows community members to challenge inequitable social structures to create a more inclusive society as well as to proactively facilitate intercultural dialogues. A multidimensional understanding of community media that considers outward and inward perspectives, as well as proactive and reactive actions, is depicted in Table 1.

4. Methodology

In Chiang Mai, there are more than 150,000 Shan migrants, almost one-sixth of the city's population (Jirattikorn, 2012; Eberle & Holiday, 2011). According to Jirattikorn (2012), Chiang Mai became a main destination for Shan migrants because of "its provincial border with the Shan State in Myanmar, the language similarity between the northern Thai dialect and Shan language, and Chiang Mai's status as a metropolitan centre in the North where there is a great deal of demand for cheap labour" (p. 215-216) (See Figure 2).

As the second largest of seven ethnic minorities in Myanmar, the Shan have struggled for independence during the country's history. In addition to long-standing civil conflicts, economic hardships in Myanmar continuously motivate the Shan people to migrate to Chiang Mai (Murakami 2012). Early migrants who arrived in Thailand before the 1960s have obtained Thai citizenship, while recent migrants often hold the status of temporary or illegal (*ibid.*). As of 2015, the majority of Shan became a part of the general migrant population living and working in Thailand (IOM, 2013; IOM, 2015), which would be the case relevant to the latter. For this reason, Thai media has often described the recent migrant workers from Myanmar as illegal or a threat to national security (Sunpuwan & Niyomsilpa 2012).

According to Jirattikorn (2016), the number of the Shan migrants is expected to grow in the near future. In Thailand, Shan migrants often work on construction, agricultural, or horticultural sites if they are men, and most Shan women work as domestic workers (Map Foundation 2012; ILO 2022). It is worth noting that the number of female Shan migrant sex workers in Chiang Mai has increased especially during the recent pandemic (Jirattikorn, A., Tangmunkongvorakul, A.,

Ayuttacorn, A., Banwell, C., Kelly, M., Lebel, L., & Srithanaviboonchai, K., 2021).

Figure 2. The location of the Shan State and Chiang Mai city
(Source: Global Administrative Areas, 2016)

The methods for collecting data in the study include the following: 1) semi-structured interviews, 2) participant observation and 3) document analysis. I interviewed 23 people, and the field work continued for seven weeks. During fieldwork, participant observation was conducted to observe interactions between listeners and broadcasters taking place at the radio station and during the broadcasting.

In addition, a few relevant documents were reviewed, including the timetable, a historical background of the establishment of Map Radio and policy guidelines for volunteer broadcasters. In addition, two minutes of the listener panels were collected, which contained 15 listeners' opinions on the radio programmes. I also attended an international conference titled "Culture and Communication for Sustainable Development Goals" on 18 December 2015 where two staff broadcasters from Map Radio presented their communication strategies for migrant workers.

5. Analytical framework

According to Howley (2010), "the feeling of affinity, belonging, 'we-ness' that we share for our local neighbourhoods, ethnic communities, or nationality is articulated within and through communication" (p. 4). As an analytical lens, articulation posits three dimensions concerning the practices of community radio: process, relationship, and agency.

Process indicates the way in which two different elements are articulated together. Specifically, process explores how community members create connections within community radio to create their own public sphere, understood as an "alternative public sphere" in the current study (Fraser, 1990). Furthermore, community radio has a strong focus on "doing communication" (Atton, 2001; Howley, 2010). This is largely linked with community participation. With this in mind, the current study explores the content produced by participants as well as community participation by different action rationales.

Relationship refers to the articulated linkages within community radio across any social levels including the nation-state, a media system, a neighbourhood, civic groups and even individuals (Howley, 2010). In the current study, I pay attention to the relationship between community radio and contemporary Thai society with the purpose of exploring the outward functions of community radio.

Agency refers to "the pivotal role human actions play in articulating and rearticulating social formation" (Howley, 2010, p. 15). In other words, a form of articulation emerges when community members are empowered through their participation in community radio (Mhlanga, 2015). In the context of community radio, agency can bring about social changes by mobilising individual and collective abilities. To analyse the social consequences of community radio practices and in keeping with the multidimensionality of community media (Fleras, 2009, 2015), I adopt "articulation" as an analytical framework based on the theoretical grounds discussed.

6. Analysing Map Radio FM 99

6.1. Articulating the process of Map Radio FM 99

The Migrant Assistant Programme (Map) Radio FM 99.75 under study is the first community radio station in the Shan language in Chiang Mai. With the financial support of the Map foundation, Map Radio has been broadcasting for the migrant community in Chiang Mai since 2004. Radio programmes are broadcast in three languages: (northern) Thai, Shan and Burmese[1]. Today, Map Radio aims to be a "space where migrant workers voices and opinions can be heard by encouraging public participation and civic engagement" (Map Foundation, 2009). This highlights the desire of Map Radio to be the alternative public sphere for migrant workers.

Participation with different action rationales

Broadcasting at Map Radio is performed by both volunteer and staff broadcasters who have an average of almost six years of experience in broadcasting. All parties engage in broadcasting and their skills used for broadcasting have been largely self-managed after a short time of training.

Most volunteer broadcasters mentioned that their largest motivation was concern about migrant workers and an awareness that new Shan migrant workers need

---

[1] The Map foundation has two Map CRSs: Map Radio FM 99 in Chiang Mai and Map Radio 102.5 in the Mae Sot district of eastern Thailand. The programmes at the Mae Sot CRS are broadcast in Burmese since the migrant and refugee population in MaeSot is dominantly Burmese because of its proximity to the Myanmar border. These programmes are recorded from the MaeSot station and broadcast in Chiang Mai using online files.

specific information to properly navigate life in Thailand. One staff broadcaster mentioned during the interview that "broadcasting is my interest and I feel happy when I can help migrant workers," a sentiment shared by other volunteer broadcaster interviewees. With this in mind, it is perhaps clear that volunteer broadcasters' participation in Map Radio is largely motivated by shared experiences with and empathy for Shan migrant workers.

Map Radio allocates almost half of each broadcasting slot for phone calls from listeners. All listeners interviewed responded that they listen to Map Radio because the radio programmes provide them with useful information, including the period for visa extension, Thai migration policy changes and updated news on the Shan State in Myanmar. Furthermore, one listener mentioned, "Map Radio speaks in Shan and talks about the Shan issues which are not dealt with on Thai radio." This highlights the alternative nature of Map Radio in comparison with mainstream media not spoken in minorities' languages.

Interestingly, most volunteer and staff broadcasters were previous listeners of Map Radio. One staff broadcaster said, "I was a listener before and listened to songs and migrant issues from the Map Radio. I also talked with broadcasters through the phone-in programme." Considering such sentiments, it is possible that participants' experiences as listeners through access to and interaction with media content encouraged them to become broadcasters, as emphasised by Carpentier (2011).

Namely, their participation *through* radio programmes and supported participation *in* Map Radio served as motivators. Furthermore, staff broadcasters attend regular meetings as well as participate in a monthly listener panel to discuss overall issues related to the management of Map Radio and content of its radio programmes. These participants' action rationales, which include different motivations and activities, are summarised in Table 2 below.

Participants with different action rationales	Motivation	Activities
Listeners	- Information on Thai migration policies, visa extension - News on the Shan State	- Phone-calls - Listener panel
Volunteer broadcasters	- Interest in broadcasting and volunteering - Concern and awareness about Shan migrant workers and their situation in Thailand - Former listeners - Recommendations from the Shan community	- Broadcasting - Monthly broadcasters meeting
Staff broadcasters	- Work responsibility - Individual interests - Concern and awareness of Shan migrant workers and their situation in Thailand	- Broadcasting - Monthly broadcasters meeting - Regular staff meeting

Table 2. Participants' action rationales at Map Radio

Content

At Map Radio, most programmes are broadcast in the Shan language, accounting for 53 out of 77 hours of broadcasting per week. Programmes in Thai (20 hours) and programmes in Burmese (4 hours) are also broadcast. The programmes can be categorised into nine themes: religion, culture, health, migrant workers, youth, women, media, news, and others.

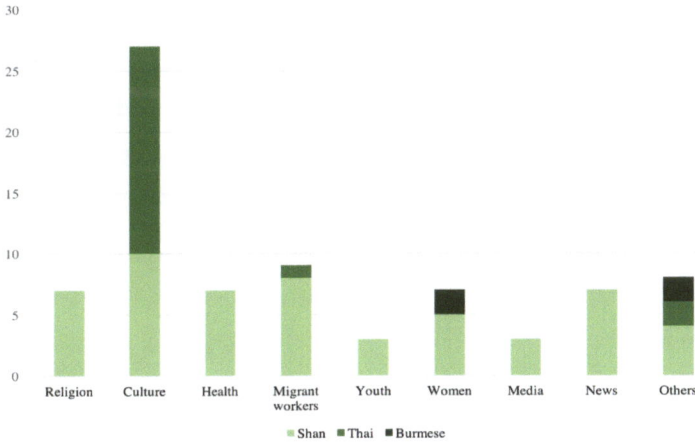

Figure 3. Broadcast hours per week according to theme and language

As seen in Figure 3, programmes on culture take up the largest share of broadcasting hours (27) followed by migrant workers (9), other (8), health (7), religion (7), news (7), women (6), youth (3) and media (3). Interestingly, cultural programmes broadcast in Thai have more broadcasting hours than those in Shan.

During my observation of *Shan Tea Table Programme*, the Shan singer Nang Hseng Lu from the Shan State was invited to the programme to celebrate the Shan New Year. Such flexibility was often observed during Shan festivals and other Shan community activities. Arguably, the content produced by Map Radio is to a large extent culturally motivated with a strong focus on the Shan community. Nonetheless, some of the content produced in Thai and Burmese also enables community members to experience a sense of multicultural belongingness in Thai society. This demonstrates the "normative legitimacy" of Map Radio as an alternative public sphere characterised by an inclusive nature regarding varying ethnicities, as explained by Fraser (1990). However, it is notable that at Map Radio, political opinions cannot be expressed during broadcasting because of the

37

strict censorship from the Thai military. Instead, only political news with exact sources can be broadcast. One staff broadcaster notes, "…we should follow Thai rules and policies since we are in Thailand. If not, we will be closed down. We just mention Thai policies related to migrant workers, not really opinions, just facts, exactly what happened."

In considering this sentiment, political discourses arising from Map Radio is not arguably accompanied by the formation of a public opinion. This indicates the diminished functionality of Map Radio as an alternative public sphere particularly for political efficacy, which delivers the will of the community as a form of civil society, as described by Fraser (1990). This also suggests a diminished potential for Map Radio to be an influential and strong public sphere in Thai society.

6.2. Articulating relationships in Map Radio FM 99

Relationship between listeners and broadcasters

The relationship between listeners and broadcasters is primarily created through phone-in programmes. All listeners interviewed discussed a preference for calling the radio station when they listen to the radio. Listeners typically comment on the topic being discussed and they request songs. Additionally, one listener responded that 'I asked them to give educative advice to the Shan youth' (Interviewee 16, 2016). Furthermore, interactions between listeners and broadcasters take place even while music is playing during the programmes. For this reason, it can be said that during broadcasts more focus is paid to communication between listeners and broadcasters than on the broadcasting itself. This aspect reveals Map radio's support of two- way communication among participants as explained by Servaes & Malikhao (2005). Meanwhile, broadcasters described their relationships with listeners in three ways. First, they emphasize 'their horizontal way of communication in sharing opinions, feedbacks and having conversation without hierarchy with listeners' (Interviewee 7, 2015; Interviewee 8, 2015; Interviewee 10, 2015). Second, they are close to listeners 'like friends' (Interviewee 13, 2015) even though they have not met each other. Finally, their relationship is often concretized by meeting each other at Shan festivals, markets, or when listeners come visit the station (Interviewee 8, 2015; Interviewee 9, 2015; Interviewee 11, 2015). Thus, the relationships between participants often go beyond airtime and extend into their daily lives outside the station, creating community bonds.

Thai broadcasters in Thai programmes

There are five programmes broadcast in Thai on Map Radio. One Shan staff broadcaster mentioned "we try to build our relationship between Thai and Shan, and it is actually going well." From the beginning of Map Radio, a Thai broadcaster from *Thai Community Programme* has assisted in designing the broadcasting timetable with Shan community members. Her programme is currently broadcast 10 hours a week and is the biggest slot among cultural programmes as shown in Figure 3. When it comes to the participation of Thai broadcaster at Map Radio, one staff broadcaster responded, "Our Thai DJ can talk well, and she can link migrant issues with the Thai community for listeners. Even though she speaks in Thai, her information can be about the Shan, which is very good."

In fact, Thai listeners as well as Shan migrants listen to *Thai Community Programme*. Because of language similarities, Shan migrants are willing to listen to Thai programmes. In addition, one government official from the Thai immigration office broadcasts information regarding recent policy changes during

Immigration Programme for one hour per week. This programme is particularly helpful for participants' living conditions because relevant legal information is delivered. One listener mentioned this programme, suggesting "this programme is so important for us, so Map Radio should increase broadcasting time." Thai citizens' involvement with the radio station shows the intention of Map Radio to promote intercultural dialogue with Thai society. In addition, the presence of Thai broadcasters and Thai programmes at the radio station suggests that the meaning of community at Map Radio can be understood more than as simply the Shan migrant community.

Partnership with the Shan Woman's Action Network

Several partner organizations also broadcast from Map radio. As of writing this study, three partner organizations are associated with Map radio: the Shan Woman's Action Network (S.W.A.N.), Workers' Solidarity Associations (W.S.A.), and Tai (Shan) Literature & Cultural Society[5]. All three are civil society organisations based in Chiang Mai. Although these partner organizations address different topics, such as women, migrant workers, and the Shan culture, all broadcasters are Shan migrants. This demonstrates their ethnic links and collective experiences as migrants. The S.W.A.N., in particular, has been a long-term partner organization with Map radio[6]. In the times of Empowerment radio, Shan migrants from S.W.A.N. were also invited to broadcast on the station, especially on Women's Day or Independence Day (Interviewee 10, 2015). The S.W.A.N is connected to Map radio in terms of shared topics such as 'migrant workers, health, work permits, and Shan women and children' (*ibid.*). The S.W.A.N. encourages Shan women staff to participate in broadcasting as partner volunteers with the goal of helping them to be more confident while voicing their opinions in public (*ibid.*). In so far as Lewis (2008) claims collaborative partnerships with other organisations are important in that they facilitate social gains associated with community radio, the argument can be made that at Map radio, through partnerships, this social gain is created by encouraging Shan migrants to be involved in producing media content and sharing opportunities for broadcasting. This can be described as 'horizontal growth within community members' (Carpentier et al. 2003).

Strategic alliance with the National Radio Thailand Chiang Mai

In early 1990s, the Shan community was excluded from the hill tribe program of NRT Chiang Mai (Interviewee 2, 2015). Under the control of the Public Relations Department (PRD) of the Thai government (Jirattikorn 2012), the NRT is one of Thailand's main broadcasting regulators (Lewis 2006). The hill tribe program was initiated primarily as an alternative tool for disseminating Thai policy-related information in minorities' languages with the purpose of assimilating these minorities into Thai society (Jirattikorn 2012). As the Shan migrant population increased in the mid 1990s, the Shan community requested the official addition of the Shan language to this programme (*ibid.*). This may be seen as resistance by the Shan communities towards their marginalization and as an effort to integrate into the public sphere. The request was accepted in 1996 and the Shan programme started being broadcast every day for 30 minutes (Interviewee 3, 2015). Now, every Monday and Tuesday, two staff broadcasters from Map radio broadcast the Shan Programme *Knowledge of Living* for Shan migrant workers for one hour at the NRT Chiang Mai radio station with one Shan broadcaster who works for NRT Chiang Mai (Interviewee 23, 2016).

While Map radio has a limited reach of 35 kilometres because of its use of Frequency Modulation (FM), the NRT uses Amplitude Modulation (AM) (1476

AM KHz) which has 'a larger range' capable of reaching more people and on a national scale (Chandler & Munday 2011). Often, this reaches some regions in Myanmar as well as China (Interviewee 22, 2015). Accordingly, this increases listeners' chances for 'access to' and to 'interact with' media content as discussed by Carpentier (2011). Furthermore, this suggests that Map radio can possibly expand from its position in a local, micro public sphere to a meso or macro public sphere as Keane (1995) argues. One Shan broadcaster from NRT Chiang Mai mentioned,

> Sometimes when I get new information on the Thai migration policies from the government officials, I gave them to the Map radio, which is important for people there. And when I have calls from listeners asking for some help while broadcasting, I let them know about the Map radio. (Interviewee 23, 2015)

For this reason, though Map radio and NRT Chiang Mai are different sizes, they are interconnected spheres for addressing migrant issues. This is made possible because they are constructed from 'difference' as Keane (1995) notes. This difference arises from the fact that 'there are some things that NRT cannot say, but can be possible at the Map Radio, and also the other way around' (Interviewee 23, 2015). While NRT Chiang Mai mainly broadcasts recent information on Thai migrant policy, it focusses more on delivering this information rather than facilitating public discussion (*ibid.*). On the other hand, although Map radio delivers relatively little in terms of information, it is freer to discuss issues with listeners. In other words, the relationship between the two is somewhat complimentary, considering the role NRT Chiang Mai plays as an informant and Map radio plays as a space for community discussion.

However, to participate in the hill-tribe language, Map radio is required to pay money to the Thai PRD. Concerning this issue, one staff broadcaster responded, 'we had to stop the relationship with the NRT Chiang Mai for a couple of years, since we did not support their system due to the lack of transparency' (Interviewee 3, 2015). This shows that the strategic alliance between the Thai government and Map radio was not beneficial for Map radio because of a lack of respect towards Map radio from the Thai authorities. On the other hand, this also demonstrates Map radio's willingness to re-establish a relationship with NRT Chiang Mai, a process facilitated by the fluid and non-linear features of community media (Bosch 2008).

In other words, even though a strategic alliance between Map radio and NRT Chiang Mai may promote Shan migrant discourse on a national level and disseminate relevant information, this alliance itself seems to have done little to diminish antagonism towards mainstream state media, as argued by Carpentier et al. (2003).

6.3. Articulating the agency of Map Radio FM 99

At Map Radio, all participants except for one responded that they have experienced personal changes after becoming involved in broadcasting. Some broadcasters have become more confident, for instance, when speaking in public, meeting people outside and writing transcripts for broadcasting. Two broadcasters are employed or received offers for employment from broadcasting organizations. In this way, participation in Map Radio may bring about socio-economic opportunities which enable participants to actively participate in Thai society. Moreover, interactions with listeners can make broadcasters feel empowered through sharing information with listeners. For instance, one staff broadcaster responded, "I found that information I talked during the broadcasting was so useful and important for migrant workers. I think I love that. I like the interactions with listeners. I feel like I can help them."

Arguably, frequent interactions with listeners may provide opportunities for empowering broadcasters. Additionally, as discussed, most listeners listen to Map Radio to gain information about the Shan State in Myanmar as well as their life in Thailand.

Since establishing Map Radio, participants have wanted to expand their working area and the influence of the radio station beyond the Shan community in Chiang Mai. Several broadcasters noted a willingness to have an Amplitude Modulation (AM) frequency and establish a community radio station in the Shan State. Furthermore, broadcasters mentioned "we want to train Shan youth to make them become broadcasters of Map Radio." Regarding participants' collective changes, one volunteer broadcaster responded,

I think Thailand is more advanced. In the Shan State, we just started accepting the typical norms. Last time, in my programme, I talked about gender equality and discrimination. I knew that people have rights.... human, child, women's rights.... I've learned this from the community, which made us change.

As this sentiment demonstrates, such changes are made because of participants' realisations of their fundamental rights by providing and gaining information through their engagement in the community radio station. Arguably, this awareness of rights and a common social status as ethnic migrant workers strengthened participants' collective identities and can potentially facilitate collective movements in the future.

7. Conclusion

This study was conducted to explore a range of social consequences resulting from the practices of a community radio station in Chiang Mai, Thailand, to understand the role of this radio station as an alternative public sphere for the Shan migrant community in Thai society.

In this study, I have argued that Map Radio has emerged as an alternative public sphere because of an early marginalisation and exclusion of the Shan migrant community from Thai society. The content produced by Map Radio is to a large extent culturally motivated with a strong focus on the Shan community among others and mostly spoken in the Shan language, which strengthens a shared identity of the Shan migrant and maximises their participation in society through this media channel. Based on shared experiences and empathy among Shan migrant workers, it becomes clear that the radio station plays an important role of providing necessary information for new Shan migrants. However, when looking at the Shan community itself, not with the comprehensive structural viewpoint of the media landscape in Thailand, it is arguable whether Map Radio could be considered as an alternative public sphere as framed in this study. It is rather proved that Map Radio has been working as a formal public sphere for the Shan migrant community. Indeed, Map Radio has a central role for the Shan migrant community in building up their buffers and plays a significant role in their socio-cultural survival in a new land.

I have also claimed that this community is attempting to strengthen relationships with Thai and Burmese communities in addition to strengthening relations between Shan community members. The radio station achieves this through the utilisation of diverse languages and a variety of multicultural programmes and engagement of different community members. This is identified by the presence of Thai broadcasters and Thai programmes at the radio station. In this regard, it is clear that Map Radio operates both inwardly and outwardly to varying degrees according to Fleras's (2009) argument. Furthermore, I have argued that as a tool for emancipation, Map Radio empowers participants on individual and collective levels. Individually, participants have become more active, confident, and knowledgeable, in some cases increasing their socio-economic participation in Thai society. On a collective level, participants have been expected to exert collective agency by establishing radio stations in the Shan State to achieve communication rights. This clearly shows community radio is playing a role of social capital as Fleras (2009) describes.

While Map Radio seems to actively engage in creating community solidarity and cohesion, thereby constructing buffers for new Shan migrants, it is nonetheless unclear whether it proactively operates outwards beyond the community in Thailand. This may be partially explained through the insufficient political efficacy of Map Radio attributable to migrants' challenging socio-economic status along with the political environment in the country, which can be characterised as threatening. Although this restrictive political situation is also applied for other community radio stations in the country, regardless of which community they serve, I would argue that a political environment in the country which guarantees freedom of expression and communication rights may favourably increase the presence of the Map Radio as an influential and strong public sphere in Thai society. Arguably, this may further bring about positive effects on intercultural dialogues between this ethnic migrant community and current Thai society by supporting the social participation of this community and strengthening the linkage among communities.

Since the country has not recognised multiculturalism as a critical national agenda and an independent community broadcasting landscape has not been promised, discussing the social consequences of community radio might be premature. Nonetheless, the case of Map Radio provides an example of how a radio station has managed to serve an ethnic migrant community by operating their own radio station premised on community participation. Still, it remains to be seen whether this radio station can continue their inward or outward functions for this community in the long run. With this in mind, sustainability in relation to financial issues and the strategic management of participants, which may negate potential conflicts among participants with different action rationales, seems to be imperative. Even though the future of Map radio remains unknown, it is clear that Map radio as an alternative public sphere can connect the Shan migrant community with Thai society by removing barriers and creating community cohesion.

Lastly, the context where the Community Radio Station operates has been evolving due to digital transformation and an innovation of evolving technologies and the following increased online broadcasting. The Map Radio is no exception in this trend. The station has been delivering online broadcasting services through social media channels (Facebook) and also through a mobile app as a way of podcast series. In this line of thinking, understanding the changing context within which a certain community radio station operates is thus a prerequisite to facilitate a clear understanding of the current position of the radio station and a nature of the people involved, that is, community.

To uphold the protection of freedom of expression and human rights for the community members, it would be considered beneficial for the staff members of the radio station to participate in several dialogues taking place for formulating online broadcasting services of the Map Radio as digital platforms to secure public information on a regular basis (UNESCO 2023). This would help combat disinformation and address better an urgent concern for the Shan community ultimately to build inclusive and informed communities in Thailand (UNESCO 2020). In addition, this would help the radio station expand their scope of broadcasting coverage into their homeland in Myanmar, which is the southern part of the Shan state where the majority of Shan migrants living in Chiang Mai originally came from, under the condition that the collective agency within the station is well-formed. This would also ultimately influence the path to forge a better information ecosystem (UNDP 2021).

The recent political upheaval in 2021 in the country caused lots of confusion to the migrant community, which put Shan migrants at risk of abuse and exploitation because of impartial and lack of accurate information (ILO 2022). Responding to this crisis, Map Radio has been providing humanitarian assistance for such group of the stranded and vulnerable community among the Shan migrant population in Chiang Mai by sharing fact-based news subject to objectivity (VOA 2022). In amidst of the political instability and lack of information related to their safety, nevertheless, Map Radio FM 99 has been pioneering the community media landscape in Thailand, focusing on the foundation of the radio station through strong bonds and community leadership, while responding flexibly to new online services in a digital era.

References

Atton, C. (2001). *Alternative media*. London: Sage Publications.

Berrigan, F.J. (1981). *Community communications: The role of community media in development*. Paris: UNESCO.

Bosch, T. (2014). Community radio. In *The handbook of development communication and social change*. Chichester, UK: John Wiley & Sons.

Brooten, L. & Klangnarong, S. (2009). People's media and reform efforts in Thailand. *International Journal of Media & Cultural Politics, 5*(1), 103-117.

Carpentier, N. (2011). *Media and participation: A site of ideological-democratic struggle*. Bristol: Intellect Books.

Cohen, A.P. (1985). *The symbolic construction of community*. London: Routledge.

Devin Stroink, Elizabeth Edwards. (2021). Radio and audio in 2020. Journal of Radio & Audio Media 28:2, pages 344-354.

Eberle, M.L. & Holliday, I. (2011). Precarity and political immobilisation: Migrants from Burma in Chiang Mai, Thailand. *Journal of Contemporary Asia, 41*(3), 371-392.

Elaine L. (2022). People's Radio: a friend to Burmese migrant workers in Thailand, retrieved from https://labourreview.org/peoples-radio/, [Accessed 2023-01-30]

Fraser, N. (1990). Rethinking the public sphere: A contribution to the critique of actually existing democracy. *Social Text, 25*(26), 56-80.

Fraser, N. (2007). Transnational public sphere: Trans-nationalizing the public sphere: On the legitimacy and efficacy of public opinion in a post-westphalian world. *Theory, Culture and Society, 24*(4), 7-30.

Fleras, A. (2009). Theorizing multicultural media as social capital: Crossing borders, constructing buffers, creating bonds, building bridges. *Canadian Journal of Communication 34*(4), 725-729.

Fleras, A. (2015). Multicultural media in a post-multicultural Canada? Rethinking integration. *Global Media Journal: Canadian Edition, 88*(2), 25-47.

Global Administrative Areas (2016). GADM database of Global Administrative Areas, version 2.0. [Online] Retrieved from www.gadm.org.

Georgiou, M. (2005). Diasporic media across Europe: Multicultural societies and the universalism-particularism continuum. *Journal of Ethnic & Migration Studies, 31*(3), 481-498.

Habermas, J, Lennox, S, & Lennox, F. (1974). The public sphere: An encyclopedia article. *New German Critique, 3*, 49-55.

Hayami, Y. (2006). Introduction: Notes towards debating multiculturalism in Thailand and beyond. *Southeast Asian Studies, 44*(3), 283-294.

Howley, K. (Eds.) (2010). *Understanding community media*. Thousand Oaks: Sage Publications.

Hirschmeier, S., Tilly, R., & Beule, V. (2019). Digital Transformation of Radio Broadcasting: An Exploratory Analysis of Challenges and Solutions for New Digital Radio Services. *Proceedings of the Annual Hawaii International Conference on System Sciences.* https://doi.org/10.24251/hicss.2019.602

International Labour Organisation (2022) TRIANGLE in ASEAN Quarterly Briefing Note for Myanmar, ILO, [Online]. Retrieved from https://www.ilo.org/wcmsp5/groups/public/---asia/---ro-bangkok/documents/genericdocument/wcms_735107.pdf, [Accessed 2023-01-30]

International Organization for Migration. (2013). Assessing potential changes in the migration patterns of Myanmar migrants and their impacts on Thailand,

IOM, [Online]. Retrieved from

https://thailand.iom.int/sites/default/files/Resources/Publications/EN%20-%20A
ssessing%20Potential%20Changes%20in%20the%20Migration%20Patterns%20
of%20Myanmar%20Migrants.pdf, [Accessed 2020-02-29]

Jallov, B. (2012). Empowerment radio. *Appropriate Technology, 39*(2), 67.

Jirattikorn, A., Tangmunkongvorakul, A., Ayuttacorn, A., Banwell, C., Kelly, M., Lebel, L., & Srithanaviboonchai, K. (2021). Shan Migrant Sex Workers Living with HIV Who Remain Active in Sexual Entertainment Venues in Chiang Mai, Thailand. *Journal of Racial and Ethnic Health Disparities, 9*(5), 1616–1625. https://doi.org/10.1007/s40615-021-01101-9

Jirattikorn, A. (2012). Brokers of nostalgia: Shan migrant public spheres in Chiang Mai, Thailand. *Living Intersections: Transnational Migrant Identifications In Asia*, February, 213-234.

Jirattikorn, A. (2016). Radio and non-citizen public sphere: Exploring Shan migrant public sphere in the city of Chiang Mai, Thailand. *South East Asia Research, 24*(1), 99-117.

Jory, P. (2000). Multiculturalism in Thailand. *Harvard Asia-Pacific Review*, 4(1), 18-22.

Kabeer, N. (2012). Empowerment, citizenship and gender justice: A contribution to locally grounded theories of change in women's lives. *Ethics & Social Welfare, 6*(3), 216-232.

Khwaja, A.I. (2005). Measuring empowerment at the community level: An economist's perspective. *Measuring empowerment: Cross-disciplinary perspectives (pp.* 267-284), Washington DC: The World Bank.

Klangnarong, S. (2009). A decade of media reform in Thailand. *Media Development, 56*(1), 24-28.

Leal, S. (2009). Community radio broadcasting in Brazil: action rationales and public space. *Radio Journal: International Studies in Broadcast & Audio Media, 7*(2), 155-170.

Mhlanga, B. (2015) The return of the local: Community radio as dialogic and participatory. In A. Salawu & M. Chibita (Eds.), *Indigenous language media: Language politics and democracy in Africa* (pp. 87-112). London: Palgrave Macmillan.

Map Foundation. (2009). For the health and knowledge of ethnic labour, map foundation. Retrieved from http://www.mapfoundationcm.org/eng/index.php/programs/map-multi-media, [Accessed 2020-02-29]

Map Foundation. (2015). Timetable of map radio FM 99 MHZ. Retrieved from .http://www.mapradio.org/pdf/Android%20update%20brochure%20-%20July%202015%20[FRONT].pdf, [Accessed 2020-02-29]

McDonald, K., & Chignell, H. (2023). The Bloomsbury Handbook of Radio. Bloomsbury Publishing USA.

Meadows, M. (2015). Blackfella listening to blackfella: Theorising indigenous community broadcasting, In C. Atton (Ed.), *The routledge companion to alternative and community media*. London: Routledge.

Murakami. T. (2012). Buddhism on the border: Shan Buddhism and trans-border migration in northern Thailand. *Southeast Asian Studies, 1*(3), 365-393.

Rodríguez, C. (2008). *Radical media*. Hoboken, NJ: John Wiley & Sons, Inc.

Sen, A. (2001). *Development as freedom*. Oxford: Oxford University Press.

Siriyuvasak, U. (2009). Conditions for media reform in Asia. *Media Development, 56*(1), 19-24.

Sunpuwan, M. & Niyomsilpa, S. (2012). Perception and misperception: Thai public opinions on refugees and migrants from Myanmar. *Journal of Population and Social Studies 21*(1), 47-58.

UNDP (2021) UNDP joins the Digital Public Goods Alliance to accelerate inclusive digital transformation (online) Retrieved from https://www.undp.org/news/undp-joins-digital-public-goods-alliance-accelerate-inclusive-digital-transformation, [Accessed 2023-01-23]

UNESCO (2020) UNESCO and UNDP launch consultation on the impact of disinformation (online) https://www.unesco.org/en/articles/unesco-and-undp-launch-consultation-impact-disinformation

UNESCO (2023) Global Conference, 22-23 February 2023: Regulating Digital Platforms for Information as a Public Good, Retrieved: https://unesdoc.unesco.org/ark:/48223/pf0000382949, [Accessed: 2023-01-30]

UN Women. (2021). How women migrants in Thailand are stopping trafficking and gender-based violence in their communities, (Online) Retrieved from: https://asiapacific.unwomen.org/en/news-and-events/stories/2021/07/feature-women-migrants-in-thailand-are-stopping-trafficking-and-gender-based-violence, [Accessed 2023-01-30]

Vatikiotis, P. (2005). Communication theory and alternative media. *Westminster Papers in Communication and Culture, 2*(1), 4-29.

Voice of Asia (2022) In Myanmar, Young Men Face Stark Choice: Join Army or Face Heavy Fines. Retrieved: https://www.voanews.com/a/in-myanmar-young-men-face-a-stark-choice-join-the-army-or-face-heavy-fines/6669525.html, [Accessed: 2023-01-30]

Wijesingha, J. S. J. (2016). *The location of the Shan state and Chiang Mai city*, map. Retrieved from https://pdfs.semanticscholar.org/85de/60d6d4f44b3af691eb28275870c8673a4a6a.pdf, [Accessed 2020-02-29]

www.ingramcontent.com/pod-product-compliance
Lightning Source LLC
Chambersburg PA
CBHW040126270326
41926CB00034B/25